learn to
sleep

how to get
the sleep you need
and deserve

Nicola Jenkins

p

This is a Parragon Book
First published in 2003

PARRAGON
Queen Street House
4 Queen Street
Bath BA1 1HE, UK

Produced by
THE BRIDGEWATER BOOK COMPANY LTD

Photography by
MIKE HEMSLEY AT WALTER GARDINER PHOTOGRAPHY

Photographic models:
ADAM CARNE, ANNE POWER

Hardback ISBN: 1-40542-297-1
Paperback ISBN: 1-40542-299-8

Printed in China

contents

what happens
when we sleep

⋀ *Night shift*
As we sleep, we relax,
our breathing is
regulated and we start
repairing any damage
to the body's systems.

We spend a third of our lives sleeping, yet within our lifetimes, most people will experience problems with sleep at some time or another, whether it involves nightmares, snoring, restless partners, jet lag or wakeful children. When faced with any or all of these for extended periods of time, a good night's sleep is suddenly all that we long for. If you have picked up this book, no doubt you, or someone you care for, are having difficulty sleeping. In the following pages you will find a range of practical and effective steps that you can take to improve the quality and amount of sleep you get.

Recent research suggests that our nervous systems are very active both when we are awake and when we are sleeping. The nervous system, like many busy organizations, works in shifts. Certain parts of the brain are active during our waking hours and are responsible for receiving, processing and transmitting messages, and for producing specific neurotransmitters (chemicals that help to pass on the messages) that help to keep us active. When we are awake, adenosine, a chemical that causes drowsiness, builds up in our blood. As we fall asleep, so the nervous system's 'night shift' takes over and different nerve cells start working, sending out messages that help us to break down the adenosine, to relax the muscles, to regulate the breathing and repair any damage to the body's systems.

Stages of sleep

There are two main types of sleep, Non-rapid Eye Movement sleep and Rapid Eye Movement sleep, called NREM and REM sleep for short. As we sleep, we move between these types of sleep in cycles. A full sleep cycle takes between 90 and 120 minutes on average, with the first sleep cycles of the night containing relatively short periods of REM sleep and longer periods of deep sleep. As morning approaches, REM sleep periods increase in length and deep sleep decreases. Healthy sleep requires a balance of the two types of sleep. How the sleeper responds to being woken often indicates what stage of sleep they were in when they were awoken.

Within NREM sleep, there are four distinct stages to sleep. The different stages of sleep are only identifiable using an EEG (electroencephalogram) to look at the electrical impulses produced by the brain during sleep.

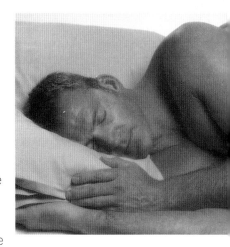

∧ *Stage 1 sleep*
Waking at this time can feel as if you are falling off a cliff.

STAGE 1. As the sleeper begins to relax, this stage lasts between one and seven minutes and takes up about five per cent of our sleeping time. When woken from this stage, you often get a sense of falling, or you may 'jump' on waking.

STAGE 2. We spend 50 per cent of our sleep in Stage 2 sleep. At this stage, eye movements stop and brain waves slow down. Each Stage 2 cycle lasts approximately 30 minutes.

STAGES 3 AND 4. These stages are only distinguishable from each other by the amount and kind of brain waves shown on the EEG. These stages make up what is called 'deep sleep', when it is difficult to wake the sleeper. There is no movement or muscle activity, and people waking at this time are often disorientated. This is also the time at which children are likely to wet the bed or experience night terrors or sleepwalking.

Cell growth and repair is increased during deep sleep, whilst your emotional processing and decision-making abilities are less active, suggesting that a night to 'sleep on it' allows you to view problems with a fresh, more objective eye, as well as allowing you your beauty sleep.

REM SLEEP

We spend 20 per cent of our sleep in REM sleep. At this time, breathing becomes shallow and irregular, the eyes move quickly, the limbs may be temporarily paralyzed, heart rate and blood pressure rises and dreams occur. The first REM period happens about 70–90 minutes after falling asleep. REM sleep stimulates the brain regions used for learning, which may be why infants spend so much time in REM sleep.

How much sleep do you need?

The amount of sleep you need varies with age and health. Infants need around 16 hours a day, teenagers around 9 hours, and most adults about 7 to 8 hours, although this can vary from 5 to 10, according to the person and their situation. Women during

the first three months of a pregnancy will need an extra few hours of sleep each night. As you get older, the amount of time you spend in deep sleep diminishes, with people over the age of 65 often reporting that they sleep lightly or not at all during the night. Although age will decrease the amount of deep sleep you get, disturbed sleep in older people is often linked to other conditions or to certain medications. Whilst it is possible to get used to managing on less sleep, lack of sleep will affect your moods, concentration, memory, and your reflexes – don't expect to perform at your best if you aren't getting the kind or amount of sleep your body desires.

Sleep and your biological clock

Without access to a watch, your body responds to light by making you feel either alert or drowsy as the day progresses. Light entering your eyes triggers a message sent via the brain to the pineal gland, which responds by slowing or stopping its production of the hormone melatonin. Melatonin levels in the body usually increase as darkness falls, helping to make people feel drowsier. As a result, shift workers working at night are more likely to experience sleep-related problems, and are therefore also more at risk of heart, digestive and emotional problems and accidents.

∧ *Let me sleep on it*
Emotions and decision-making are put on hold during deep sleep, letting you view problems more clearly in the morning.

Melatonin is available in some countries as a non-prescription sleeping aid believed to be particularly effective in fighting jet lag. It is currently not available in the UK, as there is not enough scientific research to prove that it works predictably or effectively. Among its reported side effects are worsening fatigue and interrupted fertility.

< Nap time
Infants need around 16 hours of sleep a day, most of which is spent in REM sleep.

▼ Light sleep
People over the age of 65 often report that they manage on less sleep than when they were younger.

< Twilight
Melatonin levels rise as darkness falls, making you feel drowsy and ready to sleep.

sleep disorders

∧ *Night owl*
Night owls rarely fall
asleep before 1am,
and love long lie-ins
at the weekend.

Troubled sleep can affect not only the sleeper, but all those around them, whether it involves loud snoring keeping partners awake; regular nightmares making children afraid to fall asleep; sleepwalking where you may put yourself or others at physical risk; or chronic insomnia, where you may lose confidence in your ability to sleep soundly. All sleep disorders will respond to some forms of treatment. Take time to identify the disorder you are experiencing and to work out why you have it.

ADVANCED SLEEP PHASE SYNDROME (ASPS) 'MORNING LARKS'

> Difficulty staying awake until bedtime and waking earlier than desired. The sleeper will get a normal amount of sleep. Daytime activities are not affected, but social situations are. It is sometimes confused with depression, since the sleeper will be going to sleep before 9 pm and waking between 1 and 3 am, and no later than 5 am. Light therapy and a slow alteration of the sleep schedule achieve good results.

BRUXISM

> Grinding or clenching of the teeth or jaw during sleep, which may cause abnormal wear or damage to the teeth, and jaw muscle and joint discomfort. There may also be other sleep disorders present. Relaxation techniques, facial massage, and wearing dental guards at night can all help (see page 23).

DELAYED SLEEP PHASE SYNDROME (DSPS) 'NIGHT OWLS'

> The sleeper is unlikely to fall asleep before 1 or 2 am. Unless another sleep disorder is present, he or she will get good quality sleep, although there may be difficulties waking in the morning. Sufferers may be sleepy during the day and will enjoy sleeping in at weekends for at least ten hours. This disorder responds to lifestyle changes, light therapy and slowly readjusting the sleep schedule until the desired pattern is reached.

HYPERSOMNIA

> Excessive sleepiness, prolonged sleep, difficulty waking and excessively deep sleep, all of which must be present for at least six months. This usually develops before age 25. Changes in lifestyle, behaviour, the use of stimulants, including alcohol and caffeine, avoiding shift work and limiting naps to 45 minutes can all help alleviate this disorder.

INSOMNIA

> Falls into three categories – transient (for a few nights), short term (for two to four weeks) and chronic (lasting over a month, happening most nights). It may be linked to stress, jet lag, environmental discomfort, side effects from medication, diet or physical/emotional changes in lifestyle.

⋀ *Morning lark*
Morning larks are up at the crack of dawn, if not earlier, and may have problems staying awake for social engagements in the evening.

JET LAG

> Disrupted sleep pattern as a result of air travel to new time zones. This responds to changes in diet, light therapy, melatonin supplements (not available in the UK), improving your sleep habits before and after flying and essential oils.

NARCOLEPSY

> Frequent attacks of REM sleep during the day that can last from several seconds to half an hour. The sleeper may lose muscle control and experience hallucinations, or may experience temporary paralysis on reawakening and disrupted sleep at night. Sleep attacks often happen following strong emotions of either joy or anger. This is usually controlled with stimulants, antidepressants and naps.

∧ Naps
There is nothing wrong in taking short naps during the day. For certain conditions, such as narcolepsy, they can be beneficial.

NIGHT TERRORS

> Sudden arousal from deep sleep often screaming and showing signs of intense fear. The sleeper will not remember the events that occurred during the episode, showing signs of confusion instead. When this occurs more than once a week or is associated with injury to the sleeper or to others, seek your doctor's advice.

NIGHTMARE

> A long frightening dream that awakens the sleeper. It is different to night terrors in that the dreams and the emotions experienced can be remembered in detail and, unlike night terrors, nightmares occur during REM sleep, not deep sleep.

NOCTURIA

> Need to urinate frequently in the night. The best way to alleviate this is to drink fluids more often in the morning and early afternoon and limit the amount of liquid drunk in the late afternoon and evening.

PERIODIC LIMB MOVEMENT

> The limbs jerk repeatedly during sleep, as often as every 20 to 40 seconds, causing repeated awakening and poor quality sleep. See your doctor for advice.

REM BEHAVIOUR DISORDER

> When the sleeper acts out dramatic or violent dreams during REM sleep. This may involve shouting, grunting, talking and movement, including periodic limb movement.

RESTLESS LEG SYNDROME

> Unpleasant crawling sensation on the legs, which is relieved by movement. This leads to the constant moving of the legs during the day and insomnia at night. It is most common in the elderly, but can occur at any age and has been linked to pregnancy, diabetes and anaemia. Seek your doctor's advice.

SLEEP APNOEA

> Very common and often undiagnosed condition, in which breathing is interrupted during sleep. Falling oxygen levels cause the brain to wake the sleeper in order to get breathing started again. Symptoms involve loud interrupted snoring, excessive daytime sleepiness, irritability, obesity, morning headaches, loss of interest in sex, and loss of concentration or memory. Mild versions can be overcome with weight loss and by not sleeping on the back; more severe versions respond to devices that force air through the air passages or by surgery. Sedatives or sleeping pills that could prevent the sleeper from waking to breathe should be avoided.

SLEEPWALKING

> Usually (but not exclusively) occurs in children, and involves them walking or moving about whilst asleep (usually in the first third of their night's sleep). Avoid situations that make them overtired and consider calming bedtime rituals, moving any hazardous objects in the bedroom, and hypnosis. Where the sleepwalker is regularly leaving the house during sleep, or potentially hurting him- or herself or others, seek professional help.

SNORING

> Initially look at methods to prevent the person from sleeping on his or her back, reducing alcohol and sedative intake, losing weight and making other lifestyle changes.

∨ *Silent night*
If you snore, lie on your side and not on your back to ensure a good night's sleep.

ten steps to a good night's sleep

Poor quality sleep is a very personal issue; no one except you really understands how much it affects you. Finding an effective personal solution may involve some experimentation. Each of the following suggestions can make a big difference, but they work best if you adopt a holistic approach – consider your physical, mental, emotional and environmental circumstances and how you could change them to promote good sleep.

⋀ Environmental harmony
Clean, sweet-smelling bed linens, fragranced with sedating essential oils, aid sleep.

1 Change your exercise pattern

Exercise helps you to burn off excess energy and takes your mind off worries. Aerobic exercise is particularly useful at helping to make you tired enough to switch off. As you exercise, you also release endorphins – another set of neurotransmitters – which help to make you feel good, ease pain, and can help to reduce any worries to a more manageable level. However, vigorous exercise only a few hours before sleep is not conducive to a good night's sleep.

CHOOSE A VARIED PROGRAMME. Exercise should be something to look forward to, relaxing and enjoyable, and not a chore. If you need to keep fit but don't enjoy the gym, why not try other activities? Cycling (outside rather than inside), horse-riding, ice-skating, roller-blading and country walks can all be built in to weekend activities if your weekdays are full.

Types of exercise

✗ *Avoid aerobic or strenuous exercise within three hours of your bedtime. It will raise your heart rate and make you more alert.*

✓ *Do any vigorous exercise earlier in the day, ideally before work. This will help to wake you up, get your energy and appetite moving and sharpen your mind. If you can't avoid doing strenuous exercise late in the evening, follow it with a warm shower, bath, sauna or something similar to help you wind down.*

✗ *Try to avoid alcohol, stimulants or spicy foods after exercise.*

ENGAGE IN EXERCISES DESIGNED TO CALM THE MIND IN THE EVENINGS. You could try yoga, gentle swimming, Tai Chi or Chi Qong.

GET OUT IN THE SUNLIGHT EVERY DAY. Walking for 20 minutes in the fresh air will lift your spirits. Do some kind of aerobic exercise for at least 20 minutes every day, or for 45 minutes three times a week.

≪ *Calm the mind*
Tai chi in the evening prepares the body for sleep.

≪ *Energize*
Aerobic exercise is a great way of waking yourself up in the morning.

2 Change your sleeping environment

In order to get a good night's sleep, you need to be completely comfortable with your bedroom, so that simply entering the room helps you to relax and prepares your mind and body to rest for the night. The following hints and tips are easy to implement and can make a profound difference:

MOVE ELECTRICAL GOODS. Alarm clocks, telephones and other electrical goods give off electrical currents to which some people are particularly sensitive. If you need to have electrical goods near the bed, make sure that the cables don't run underneath or behind it.

TAKE THE TV OUT OF THE BEDROOM. In addition to adding electrical currents in the bedroom, action-packed television shows can be too noisy and mentally stimulating.

CHANGE THE ROOM TEMPERATURE. During REM sleep, it is more difficult to regulate body temperature, which can cause you to wake up shivering or sweating. Consider increasing central heating use when the weather is cold and installing air conditioning or fans in hot weather.

CHANGE YOUR NIGHTWEAR. In cold weather, the feet and the head are the parts of the body that lose the most heat, so warm socks or a cotton head scarf can help if you feel the cold. Whatever the temperature, cotton nightwear is best.

CHANGE YOUR BEDDING. Consider using multiple, thin layers of bedding (such as sheets, throws or blankets), which can be added as necessary. If you tend to sweat heavily at night, change to natural materials such as cotton sheets. Clean sheets can also help you to relax and prepare for sleep.

REMOVE CLUTTER FROM THE BEDROOM. This is especially important if you find that your sleep is shallow, your mind is racing or if you are prone to sleepwalking.

COVER ANY MIRRORS THAT FACE THE BED. This Feng Shui tip is extremely effective if you are prone to light sleeping or insomnia. Movement reflected in a mirror could subconsciously raise sleepers.

<< Static
Move electrical goods away from the bed if you suspect you are sensitive to electrical currents.

< Natural fibres
Cotton, flannel or silk nightwear are most effective at keeping your body temperature stable.

< Fresh air
Airing the bedroom regularly increases oxygen supply and makes it a more restful and inviting environment.

CHOOSE DARK WINDOW DRESSINGS. Buy the darkest curtains or blinds that you can, to ensure that the room remains as dark as possible for sleeping in.

CHANGE YOUR MATTRESS. Buying a new mattress, or even turning the mattress over, can make a big difference if you are restless at night or wake up with back pain.

AIR THE ROOM REGULARLY. Allowing air to circulate through the room regularly helps to keep the environment clear and removes stale odours. Air fresheners, regular cleaning and even using sedating essential oils (see page 31) to fragrance the bedroom all help make it more conducive to a good night's sleep.

Alarm clocks

Choose your alarm clock with care. Loud alarms will wake you suddenly and may cause you to jump. Try one that will attract your attention but wake you up without startling you, such as a clock set to play soothing music. You could invest in one of the new light-box alarm clocks that gradually increase the amount of light in the room as you are due to wake up and decrease it at bedtime. These are particularly effective if you find your moods change with the seasons and if you are trying to readjust your sleep schedule.

3 Develop bedtime rituals

No matter how simple a bedtime ritual or habit appears, subconsciously your body recognizes it as a sign to prepare for sleep. Your nervous system will start sending out the signals that tell the 'day shift' to come off duty.

PREPARE FOR TOMORROW. Prepare anything you need for the morning, including packing bags, making lunches, ironing clothes or similar. This will stem a panic in the morning and stop night-time worrying.

TAKE A WARM BATH. A good soak can relax both body and mind. Make sure the water is not too hot, since this can raise your heart rate, which is not conducive to sleep. Try adding essential oils to your bath (see page 31), Epsom salts, or a relaxing bubble bath blend.

DON'T LIE IN BED AWAKE. If you are unable to fall asleep within half an hour, avoid watching the clock, get out of bed and find something to do. Don't return to bed until you are tired.

∧ Preparation
Have everything ready for the morning to prevent nightly worrying and morning panic.

> Warm water
For a soothing evening, try two drops each of Roman chamomile, vetiver and orange essential oils in a full bath.

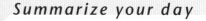

Summarize your day

Many highly organized individuals develop a habit of writing diaries or even lists at the end of the day. This technique allows you to mentally put to rest the day's events, listing all the things you need to prepare for in the days to come. Delegating your worrying to paper should calm restless thoughts.

LOWER THE LIGHTS BEFORE BEDTIME. Lowering the lighting in the room you are sitting in at least two hours before going to bed creates a more relaxed atmosphere.

LEAVE WORRIES AT THE BEDROOM DOOR. Ensure that anything representing what worries you is left outside the

bedroom. People working from home are also advised to keep computer equipment or work paraphernalia out of the bedroom, or, if this isn't possible, to tidy it out of sight at the end of the day.

RELAX BEFORE BED. Try to avoid working or carrying out mentally challenging tasks at least two hours before bedtime. Generally you will not be performing at your best at this time of the day anyway.

USE THE BED JUST FOR SLEEPING (AND SEX). As far as possible avoid using the bed for any other activities. If sex has become problematic, perhaps as a result of a medical condition or high levels of stress, it can be an idea to refrain from using the bed for sex for the short-term as well. Using the bed just for sleeping will mean that you will automatically associate it with sleep.

∨ *Essential support*

Particularly comforting and sedating essential oils include sandalwood, marjoram, yarrow, lavender, rose and patchouli.

∢ *Just for sleep*

Keep your bed just for sleeping in. Avoid anything exciting, stressful or work related in the bedroom.

4 Engage in meditation or mind exercises

Mental exercises can help to clear the mind of any fears or anxieties. By concentrating on something else, such as your breathing, or on slowly relaxing every muscle in your body, you help to put those worries where they belong – on the back burner until you are ready and willing to deal with them.

PRACTISE A DEEP BREATHING EXERCISE. Throughout this exercise, concentrate on your breathing. Breathe in slowly, pause, then slowly exhale, pause again. Repeat at least ten times. Make sure that you are breathing from your diaphragm, keeping it relaxed and rhythmic. If you are breathing in deeply from your diaphragm, your belly will rise higher than your chest when you are lying on your back.

LEARN PROGRESSIVE MUSCLE RELAXATION. Concentrate on slowly relaxing every muscle in your body. For best effects, lie on your back and imagine the muscles relaxing one by one, beginning with the muscles in your feet and legs, and slowly moving up the body until you reach the neck and facial muscles.

PRACTISE GUIDED IMAGERY (SEE BOX). Visualize the most relaxing and comfortable place you have ever been, whether it is a real place or one you imagine – perhaps a warm beach with a gentle breeze rocking your hammock, or floating in a boat in the centre of a quiet lake. Concentrate on re-creating every single detail of the place and how you feel about it in your mind. Put yourself in the picture and visualize yourself falling asleep in complete comfort.

⋀ *Meditation*
Mind calming exercises can take place anywhere that is peaceful, where you are unlikely to be disturbed.

VISUALIZATION EXERCISE

Do this exercise sitting up before going to bed or in bed lying on your back. Make yourself comfortable, ideally with your back straight. Make sure that you are fully relaxed and will not be distracted. Close your eyes and slow your breathing down. Count 15 slow inhalations before you start.

Imagine walking along a forest path. The day is warm; dappled light comes through the trees and the sun is shining. Feel your muscles relaxing. You become aware that you are carrying a heavy rucksack on your back and, as you continue to walk, it feels as if it is becoming heavier. This rucksack contains all the problems that have been weighing you down lately. As you become aware of the rucksack, the forest path opens up to run alongside a beautiful pond. You stop, take the rucksack off your back and drop it on the little beach you find there. Then you swim in the warm waters of the pond. As you emerge from the water, you find that someone has unrolled your sleeping bag. Your rucksack is gone, but a note on your bedding reads 'we have taken your problems away to be cleaned this evening and will return them in a more manageable state along with workable solutions in the morning. Rest easy until then.'

Comforted, climb into the bedding and drift off to sleep.

◄ *Visualization*
Imagine yourself in the most tranquil environment you have ever seen.

◄◄ *Progressive relaxation*
Let your muscles relax and grow heavy, starting at your toes and gradually moving towards your face.

REPEAT A MANTRA. If you have worked with meditation before and been taught the use of a mantra (a key word or phrase to focus the mind), use it to help you sleep, whilst concentrating on your breathing. It will encourage your body to remember the deep sense of relaxation that it achieves in meditation. If you haven't used a mantra before you could try 'So-Haam', saying 'So' to yourself on inhalation and 'Haam' on exhalation. Make the exhalation longer than the inhalation.

TAKE UP MEDITATION CLASSES.
Meditation can be extremely effective in aiding relaxation. Contact local colleges, community centres and health centres for details of meditation classes in your area.

5 Change your diet

Food and medicines can alter the balance of chemicals within your body, and have the potential to alter how wakeful or drowsy you feel and to affect the quality of your sleep. The most likely food culprits are caffeine, alcohol, nicotine, decongestants, diet pills and antidepressants. Generally, these substances seem to reduce the amount of REM sleep you get, regardless of whether they function as stimulants or not. The most obvious answer is to cut them out completely. Unfortunately, giving these substances up is neither easy nor quick, and is not necessarily the most effective way of improving your sleep. A more balanced approach can get you what you want without forcing you to make the major changes involved in, for instance, giving up smoking, until or unless you are ready for it. As in dieting, a slow, steady approach is more likely to produce long-term change.

➤ *Health drink*
Drinking a glass of water or fruit juice before a cup of coffee or tea can help to alleviate some of the negative effects of caffeine.

▼ *Nightcap*
A glass of milk before bed will help you sleep well.

CUT DOWN ON CAFFEINE. Drink a glass of water or fruit juice before every cup of caffeine-related substance you have (this includes tea, coffee and carbonated soft drinks). Avoid all caffeine after 4pm, and, if you see no improvements, bring this time limit forward to 2pm. Try to drink no more than two cups of tea or coffee a day.

CUT DOWN ON ALCOHOL. This is particularly important in the evenings. As far as possible, reduce your alcohol intake, matching one glass of water for every alcoholic drink, and avoid alcohol for a couple of hours before your bedtime.

CUT DOWN ON CIGARETTES. This is essential in the evenings. If you smoke heavily, consider applying nicotine patches in the evening, not only to reduce cravings but to prevent you waking because of those cravings.

TRY VITAMIN SUPPLEMENTS. A general multi-vitamin will enhance your body's functioning. Additional supplements of B vitamins are particularly useful. Vitamin B6 helps to make serotonin (another neurotransmitter which produces 'feel-good' reactions); B1 relieves fatigue; Folic acid eases depression; and Vitamin C fights the physical symptoms of stress. A lack of iron in the diet has also recently been linked to poor sleep and fatigue, so if you have a history of anaemia you may want to consider an iron supplement. Magnesium is also very useful as a muscle relaxant, so if you are grinding your teeth at night or lie awake in pain as a result of muscle tension, you might consider increasing your intake of magnesium. Be careful about the amount you take, however, as large doses of magnesium or Vitamin C can relax the bowels, causing loose stools.

INCREASE YOUR WATER INTAKE. Dehydration can sometimes be linked to poor quality sleep, especially if you go to bed thirsty. It is generally recommended that you aim to drink two litres of water a day.

DECREASE LIQUID INTAKE IN THE AFTERNOON. This is only relevant if you are waking in the night in order to urinate. Don't use this as an excuse to avoid drinking enough water; simply drink more in the morning instead.

CHOOSE YOUR SNACKS WELL. Avoid late night snacks containing sweet substances, such as cereals or processed foods, since these will raise your blood-sugar levels and can lead to excessive sweating as well as light or interrupted sleep. Snacks that involve protein are more effective at aiding sleep, which is why the traditional warm milk drink at night does have a scientific basis to it.

AVOID FOODS YOU ARE SENSITIVE TO. Mild intolerances to common foods, such as dairy products, wheat, gluten (found in all grains except rice and maize), eggs and nuts are common. Reactions can include changes in emotional state, loss of sleep and itchy skin, right through to more severe digestive problems or extreme allergic reactions. If you suspect that you may have a food intolerance, try avoiding that foodstuff completely for two weeks to see what, if any, changes you notice. After two weeks, reintroduce the substance and, if it is the source of trouble, your general health and sleep will be affected immediately.

TRY HERBAL TEAS. Chamomile, valerian, melissa or orange blossom teas are particularly recommended for insomnia.

∧ *Fresh fruit*
Fruit and vegetables contain essential vitamins and minerals that aid sleep and reduce the effects of fatigue, nervous tension and anxiety.

Amino acids

Some chronic sufferers of insomnia have reported improved sleep following taking amino acid supplements L-tryptophan or 5-hydroxytryptophan. Both these amino acids are involved in the production of a protein called tryptophan found in humans and linked to good quality sleep. For best results, and especially if you want to try the amino acid supplements, contact a registered nutritionist. Appropriate guidance in the use of supplements is strongly recommended.

6

Self-massage

Massage is particularly effective at reducing anxiety, muscle stiffness and pain, all of which can keep you awake at night. Where long-term sleep problems exist, it is advisable to get regular treatments from a massage therapist, reflexologist or aromatherapist as well as trying out the simple self-help techniques listed here.

❮ 5

❯ Self massage
A head, neck and shoulder massage is an effective way to relieve muscle stiffness caused by stress and anxiety.

1. Lift up your shoulder muscles, squeezing them between your fingers and palm. This helps to warm the area and loosen up tight muscles.

2. Concentrating on one shoulder at a time, work deeply with the fingers into the muscles around your shoulder joint and over the top of your shoulders to your neck. Repeat for the other shoulder.

3. Using both sets of fingers, work in small circles up either side of your neck, to the base of your skull.

4. Rotate your thumbs in small circles along the base of the skull.

❮ 8

❮ 6

MASSAGE TO EASE BRUXISM

Work with your fingertips in small circles in three rows.

> 1) along the sides of your face from your temples down to your jaw

> 2) from under your cheekbones down to your jaw, and

> 3) from the front of your ears to just under the edge of your jaw.

You should be pressing just hard enough that the action feels like a 'good hurt', without being too painful. Do this first with your jaw closed, then with your jaw open. Try to do this for ten minutes at least twice a day to help the muscles relax. This can be done either on its own, or by using a massage lotion or oil with relaxing essential oils in it to increase the beneficial effects.

< Painful jaws
A simple self massage using small circular movements can ease a painful jaw.

5. Working from the forehead, use your fingers to move in small hooking movements from the hairline along the scalp to the base of your skull. This is a slower version of the movement you would use when shampooing your hair.

6. Massage the ears between your thumbs and forefingers.

7. Rotate your thumbs at your temples, then hook your fingers through your hair, working the area over the ears and slowly towards the base of the skull.

8. Finish by cupping your hands behind your neck and resting your skull on your hands. Let your hands take the weight so that the neck muscles can relax.

7

Experiment with natural sleeping aids

Here are some really simple aids that can help improve sleep.

PILLOWS. These are especially important if you are feeling uncomfortable in bed, perhaps as a result of an injury, chronic pain, recent weight loss or gain or a pregnancy. Choose pillows that support your head and neck comfortably and that, where possible, help to keep your spine straight. A range of shaped pillows, including extra long ones, are now available. These can help to support a pregnant woman wanting to sleep comfortably on her side. If the problem is snoring, choose a firmer pillow that will prop

the snorer's head up higher and extend the neck so that the jaw does not open fully. Sometimes more than one pillow is needed.

EAR PLUGS. If your problem lies with your partner's snoring and your partner cannot avoid sleeping on his or her back, two little foam plugs could be all that is keeping you from a better night's sleep.

ESSENTIAL OILS. All of the essential oils listed on page 31 can aid sleep. Try a couple of drops of one essential oil on a tissue placed inside a pillow case or add up to six drops to a deep bath. Halve the number of drops for children under 12 or pregnant women, and use only two drops for children under two years. The six drops can be two drops each of three oils. You can also place up to three drops of three essential oils in a vaporizer in the bedroom before going to sleep. Alternatively, visit an aromatherapist for a detailed consultation and a blend designed specifically for you and your sleeping difficulties. Visiting a professional aromatherapist is particularly important if the person having trouble sleeping is under 12 years, is pregnant or has a serious medical condition.

BACH FLOWER REMEDIES. These gentle compounds are very useful as a source of emotional support when your sleep is disturbed as a result of stress, shock, anxiety or sudden changes in your personal circumstances. A few drops of your chosen

▼ *Shaped pillows*
Different kinds of support can help you feel more comfortable or prevent a snorer from lying on his or her back.

HOMEOPATHIC REMEDIES

Available in most health shops, the following homeopathic remedies can be very useful when you have trouble sleeping:

> **ACONITE** helps to relieve anxiety and restlessness

> **PULSATILLA** is for difficulty with falling asleep

> **SULPHUR** is used where there is sleep talking or restless leg syndrome

> **NUX VOMICA** helps to relieve early waking

> **COFFEA** should be taken if you are prone to waking at around 2 or 3am, and then only doze afterwards

Contact a professional homeopath for a detailed programme of remedies specific to your personal situation.

remedy in a glass of water, taken several times a day, can ease feelings of depression, anxiety or fear to more manageable levels. Take Rescue Remedy for shock or sudden change; elm when you find responsibilities overwhelming; gorse if you are faced with hopelessness, hornbeam to relieve tiredness and lethargy; oak for times when you have kept going beyond feeling exhausted; olive if you are exhausted following either mental or physical activity; and white chestnut when your mind is unable to relax.

> *Minimum dose*
Try homeopathic remedies. Coffea, for example, is a very effective sleeping aid.

> *Flower power*
Bach Flower remedies can help to alleviate some of the causes of disturbed sleep such as shock or anxiety.

8 Make changes to your lifestyle

If sleep problems, particularly insomnia, are long standing, it can be an indication that at a subconscious level you are not happy with your existing circumstances. Change in these areas does not always have to be dramatic to make a difference to how you feel. The most important aspect is for you to work out what particular changes will have the greatest positive impact on your happiness. Make sure they are manageable. If your long-term goals are to make dramatic changes, take time out to think about what smaller steps you can take to prepare for the big change.

MANAGE YOUR TIME EFFECTIVELY. If you constantly feel harassed, you may be trying to fit too much into your week. Consider timetabling things differently so that you do not have to rush to meetings, trains or dinner. Alter the nature of the activities that you carry out at different times of the day. If you know you are least effective in the morning, this may be the best time for you to do routine tasks that do not require mental effort.

CHANGE YOUR ROUTE TO WORK. If lengthy driving is getting to you, consider altering your route to take advantage of any public transport available. Arranging a car-share with other commuters, so that your driving is limited, is also a good option.

LOOK AT WORKING FLEXIBLY. Flexible working hours, working at home and part-time work are more readily acceptable solutions in today's working environment. Even if your employer does not currently offer this, it may be a solution they would be willing to embrace. If this is something you feel strongly about, it may be an issue you want to bear in mind for future jobs.

⋀ Manage your time better
Give yourself enough time to get to meetings or to catch trains so that you are not always in a 'rush'.

➤ Change habits
Heavy, rich meals late at night do not aid digestion or sleep, so stick to simpler food.

CREATE REALISTIC DEADLINES FOR YOURSELF. When you set yourself deadlines, either at work or at home, make sure that you take into account all the various tasks and activities you are currently engaged in. Unrealistic deadlines will increase your stress levels and will most certainly affect your sleep, whether or not you choose to forego sleep in order to meet the deadline.

GET HELP IF YOU CAN. Delegating home tasks or work tasks can ease the pressure on you and make a big difference to your ability to sleep. If finances are a worry, consider bartering for assistance – for instance, trade secretarial support for digging the garden.

CONSIDER MOVING HOME. Whilst it can be an expensive undertaking, moving home is worth considering if your sleep is affected by noisy neighbours, traffic, or by extended commuting to work.

Social life

Change how you socialize. Consider limiting the number of after-work events you engage in each week, especially if they involve extensive use of alcohol or nicotine. Suggest a change of pace by including different tension-releasing activities, such as sports activities, team-building events, and trips to a spa, the cinema or theatre.

AVOID TAKING WORK HOME IN THE EVENINGS. Although this is not always possible, it can make a big difference to your peace of mind. If you must work at home, try to stop working two hours before you are due to go to sleep.

OPERATE A CLEAN-DESK POLICY. The idea of clearing the desk or the home before going to sleep is a productive bedtime ritual, even if it just means stacking things neatly for the next day.

TRY CAREER GUIDANCE COUNSELLING. Many recruitment organizations offer counselling to those facing redundancy or organizational restructuring. Regardless of whether or not you are currently in such a situation, if you are profoundly dissatisfied with the way your work is going, it may be worth taking the various aptitude tests they offer and looking at potential opportunities for a career change.

◄ *Take a break*
Manage your time effectively so that you are not constantly being harassed, and so that you are able to take regular breaks.

9 Adjust your sleep schedule

Changing your sleep schedule is an ideal way of adjusting to a new time zone in advance of your visit, as well as an essential exercise to help those with ASPS or DSPS to adjust to a more normal routine. Deceptively simple, this activity requires you to move your bedtime either forward or backward (depending on what you wish to achieve) by half an hour each night. If the problem is long-standing, adjust your schedule even more slowly. Move your bedtime only twice a week, allowing yourself to get used to the new schedule before changing it again.

Sleep schedule

Adjusting your sleep schedule does take perseverance and is particularly successful if you also combine it with:

✓ Using a light box alarm clock (See page 15)

✓ Keeping the bedroom as dark as possible

✓ Spending as much time as possible outside in natural daylight

✓ Reducing or adjusting naps taken during the daytime

✓ Finding ways of generating 'white noise' in the bedroom. White noise is a gentle hum that cuts out other noises in the house or street that could be distracting you from sleep. Air conditioners and fans work particularly well.

> Reduce naps
Reduce daytime napping as far as possible, limiting it to less than 45 minutes.

< White noise
Fans, air conditioners or ionizers are useful sources of white noise.

Seek professional help

If your sleeping problems do not respond to any of the suggestions made here, it may be time to speak to a professional. Contact your GP first, as, apart from providing any required diagnosis, he or she will often be able to refer you on to the right person very quickly.

KEEP A SLEEP DIARY. This can be extremely useful as an aid in discussing sleep problems you are experiencing with your doctor or a sleep specialist. Regardless of the type of sleeping disorder you have, include details of the times you tried to sleep, when you think you fell asleep, when you woke up, when you were supposed to be up, what woke you, any medication you are taking (and when you took it) and how you felt during the day.

SLEEP CLINIC. A trip to the sleep clinic is likely where sleep is severely disturbed, has been disturbed for a long time or where the doctor needs to confirm a diagnosis.

HYPNOTHERAPIST. Hypnotherapy is particularly recommended where nightmares, night terrors and sleep-walking exist, but can also have a profound effect where anxiety is contributing to insomnia.

DENTIST. A visit to the dentist is strongly advised if you suffer with bruxism as, in more severe cases, people have been known to break their teeth by grinding them

in their sleep. A dental guard, worn over the teeth during sleep, can help to protect the teeth and train you not to clench your jaw.

COUNSELLOR/PSYCHOTHERAPIST. Where stress, anxiety or emotional circumstances are affecting your sleep, talking to a professional counsellor can help to give you an outlet for your fears as well as advising you on methods of dealing with them more effectively.

⋀ Sleep diary
Record how and when you have difficulties sleeping. Use this diary to discuss your sleep problem with your doctor or sleep specialist.

CASE STUDY: CHRONIC SLEEP APNOEA

Stefan reports having difficulties sleeping from childhood, saying that through his adolescence he would come home from school and sleep for a few hours before going out to play rugby, after which it was unlikely that he would get to sleep again before 2 am.

"At that time it was quite normal for me to go to school with only four hours' sleep. I had trouble getting up in the morning. The problems seem to have got worse as I've got older but I didn't do anything about it until after I got married, when my snoring was driving my wife mad."

A trip to the GP led to a referral to the sleep clinic at Hammersmith Hospital in London. The tests carried out involved Stefan using a machine which measured his heart rate, his breathing, the amount of oxygen in his body and how long he spent in each stage of sleep during the course of a night. The results showed that he was waking 57 times each hour, because his breathing would stop so frequently.

∧ Stefan
Stefan has had problems sleeping soundly since childhood.

"I've now got a CPAP machine to help me sleep at night. It forces air through the airways to keep the throat open when I am sleeping. It hasn't been brilliantly successful so far, but I think that has to do with the fact that I have particularly large tonsils and frequent bouts of tonsillitis. The surgeon who is going to take them out reckons that this will make about a 30–40 per cent improvement to the sleep apnoea. I've also been told to lose weight. Alcohol makes it even worse – if I've been drinking, you don't want to be sleeping in the same room with me or possibly even on the same floor!

I want to see how much improvement occurs once I've had the tonsils out and lost the weight, but if it doesn't improve, I'm intending to go back to the sleep clinic and see if the more expensive version of the CPAP machine will make the difference. The one I have at the moment is the NHS version which has two settings – low and high pressure. Low pressure is used whilst you are falling asleep and high pressure comes online later. The more expensive version has a computer-run programme which can be personalized to your own sleeping patterns and will regulate itself on the strength of your breath, which means that it will be able to take into account your different stages of sleep and vary its activities accordingly."

SYMPTOMS OF SLEEP APNOEA

Loud snoring
Excessive sleepiness during the day
Morning headaches
High blood pressure
Sometimes overweight
Dry mouth on waking
Depression

Difficulty concentrating
Excessive sweating in sleep
Heartburn
Reduced libido
Insomnia
Restless sleep
Rapid weight gain

Sometimes linked to chronic tonsillitis, sinusitis, frequent bouts of adenoid infections or polyps in nasal passages

Too much alcohol
Alcohol increases your chances of restlessness, insomnia, and tiredness the following day.

POTENTIAL CAUSES OF CHRONIC INSOMNIA

Depression
Arthritis
Kidney disease
Heart failure
Asthma
Sleep apnoea
Restless leg syndrome
Parkinson's disease
Hyperthyroidism
Too much caffeine

Too much alcohol
Stress
Shift work
Expecting problems with sleep and worrying about it
Smoking cigarettes before sleeping
Excessive napping in the afternoon or evening
Occasional or chronic pain

Associating bed with alert activities
Osteoporosis
Heartburn
Cancer
Senile dementia
Alzheimer's disease
Incontinence
Acid reflux
Sinus pain
Cardiovascular diseases

NATURAL SEDATIVES

Benzoin (for nightmares)
Bergamot
Clary sage
Cedarwood
Coriander
Cypress (for an overactive mind, not usually sedating)

Damiana
Geranium*
German chamomile*
Jasmine
Lavender*
Lemongrass
Mandarin*
Marjoram

Melissa
Myrrh
Neroli*
Orange
Patchouli*
Petitgrain*
Roman chamomile*

Rose
Rosewood
Sandalwood*
Tangerine
Valerian
Vetiver
Yarrow
Ylang ylang

* safe to use during pregnancy or for small children, but ensure you use half the number of drops suggested. See a professional aromatherapist if you are pregnant, have a history of unstable pregnancies, are breast-feeding, on medication, have a serious medical condition, or sensitive skin

Index